student WORKBOOK

GW00888786

GCSE Schools History Project
Study in Development: Medicine
John Collingwood

Philip Allan Updates, an imprint of Hodder Education, an Hachette UK company, Market Place, Deddington, Oxfordshire OX15 0SE

Orders
Bookpoint Ltd, 130 Milton Park, Abingdon, Oxfordshire, OX14 4SB
tel: 01235 827827   fax: 01235 400401
e-mail: education@bookpoint.co.uk

Lines are open 9.00 a.m.–5.00 p.m., Monday to Saturday, with a 24-hour message answering service. You can also order through the Philip Allan Updates website: www.philipallan.co.uk

© Philip Allan Updates 2005

ISBN 978-1-84489-452-9

Printed in Spain

Hachette UK's policy is to use papers that are natural, renewable and recyclable products and made from wood grown in sustainable forests. The logging and manufacturing processes are expected to conform to the environmental regulations of the country of origin.

Contents

Introduction

This workbook is designed to help you prepare for the GCSE examination module Study in Development: Medicine. The content is divided into nine topics, each of which provides an overview of an important aspect of the history of medicine.

Each topic contains:

- **a summary of essential knowledge**, focusing on changes in beliefs and practices through time and the main factors that have influenced those changes. These summaries are not intended to cover all the details of a particular theme and should be used with your class notes and textbook.
- **questions and exercises**, which are designed to help you learn and/or revise each topic and also practise the skills that are essential for the examination:
  - the analysis and evaluation of sources
  - the writing of extended answers, using both your own knowledge and source material

Spaces are provided for your answers and give you some idea of how long each answer should be. The questions are structured so that they increase in difficulty within each topic.

Source questions

When answering source questions there are two important points to remember.

First, don't just **describe** what a written source says, or a picture shows. Try to draw an **inference** or make a **deduction** about the overall meaning or significance of the source. For example, you could be given a picture source such as the one in Topic 7, Question 16, and asked: 'What does Source A suggest about surgery in the early 1800s?' Many candidates make the mistake of just describing in detail what they can see in the picture. Better candidates start by making an inference and then referring to details to support what they have said, such as 'Source A suggests that surgery was very dangerous in the early 1800s. You can tell this because you can see...'.

Second, if the question tells you to 'use the **source** and your own **knowledge** in your answer' — then make sure you do use both. Try to get into the habit of using the source first and referring to it by name, i.e. 'Source A' or 'Source B'. This is especially important in extended answers.

Extended writing

The last questions in each topic are designed as 'extended writing' or essay exercises. You should write your answers to these questions on separate paper. Some of these final questions tell you to use the sources in that section as well as your own knowledge in writing your answer. In the examination there will be more sources available to support your arguments than the two or three provided here, but these will enable you to practise this important examination technique. You should end these answers with a separate conclusion. However, do not just summarise what you have already said; you should state an opinion in answer to the question set and support it with a strong point.

Prehistoric times

People lived a **nomadic** way of life, dominated by the constant search for food. There was no time to settle in one place or to question why things were the way they were. Consequently, there was no real progress for centuries.

These people left no written records, so our knowledge of their way of life is based on cave paintings, archaeological remains and studies made in the twentieth century of less economically developed societies like that of the Aborigines, whose traditional way of life was similar. This evidence suggests that:

- Prehistoric people had **supernatural explanations** for disease: they believed it was caused by gods or spirits.
- They used **charms** for protection against these spirits.
- They used simple tools for **trephining** to release evil spirits from the skull.
- **Medicine men** were thought to have special healing powers.
- They may have used **herbs** or plants for treating injuries, and have offered simple **sacrifices** to please the gods.

Ancient Egypt (*c.* 3000 BC–*c.* 600 BC)

Egypt was one of the first **civilisations** — places where people settled and built permanent towns and cities. This was made possible by the development of **farming**. Now that a few people could provide food for the whole community, it was possible for others to **specialise** in things like medicine. As a result, some new ideas were developed.

- There was a new theory of disease based on the idea that the body had many **channels** — like the River Nile and the irrigation channels that came from it. Some believed that illness happened when some of these channels got blocked (just like the Nile's irrigation channels). This led to new treatments, such as **purging** with laxatives, **bloodletting** and enforced **vomiting**.
- Many Egyptians, especially priests, believed in high standards of **cleanliness**, but this was mainly for religious reasons. The rich had simple toilets, but no drainage systems.
- There were some doctors, but their treatments were based mainly on **spells and magic potions**.
- **Mummification** of bodies led to greater knowledge of the human body and its organs, but did not increase understanding of how these organs worked.
- People began to **write down** ideas about treatments and spells on papyrus documents.

However, many old ideas continued alongside the new ideas. For example:

- Most ancient Egyptians still believed that **gods**, such as Sekhmet, could cause or cure disease.
- **Charms** were worn to scare off evil spirits that brought disease.
- **Herbs** were sometimes used for treatments. Some of these were very effective.

Ancient Greece (*c.* 600 BC–*c.* 200 BC)

The Greeks, like the Egyptians, were civilised in the sense that they lived in towns and cities. Some important new ideas developed at this time because the Greeks traded with many countries and picked up knowledge from them. Ancient Greece was also quite a rich society and people at 'the top' had many slaves. This meant that they had time to think about and develop new ideas. The Greeks also had enquiring minds and wanted to understand the natural world better. They developed new ideas in many areas, including maths and science as well as medicine.

- The most important development was the **theory of the four humours** because it was the first widely accepted explanation for disease based on natural and not supernatural causes. The theory was accepted by doctors for another 1,500 years and so greatly influenced how people were treated for illness during this time. According to the theory, illness developed when there was too much or too little of one of the four humours in the body — black bile, yellow bile, phlegm and blood. Treatments were also natural: patients were often told to rest, take care over their diet and let nature take its course. If this did not work, a doctor might try to restore the balance of the humours by, for example, bloodletting. The balance of the humours was thought to be affected by the seasons: for example, people seemed to have too much phlegm during the winter months and this was thought to cause illness.
- Hippocrates insisted on high standards of behaviour from doctors (they were expected to take the **Hippocratic Oath**).
- Medical books were produced so that knowledge and ideas could be passed on to each new generation of doctors (the **Hippocratic Collection**).
- Doctors were taught to observe patients carefully, record their symptoms and learn to forecast how an illness would develop (**clinical observation**).

- Hippocratic doctors also believed that care over diet and exercise would maintain good health.
- Although they were more 'scientific', Greek doctors depended on argument and discussion when forming new ideas. They did not use experiments for proof like modern scientists.

These new ideas did not mean that old ideas disappeared. Both continued side by side.

- Most ancient Greeks still believed that gods and goddesses caused things to happen. **Asclepios** was a god of healing and many Greeks preferred to go to a temple (the Asclepion) rather than to a doctor. Here, they believed that Asclepios would visit them in the night with his daughters Panacea and Hygeia, and cure them. People who recovered from an illness left stone inscriptions behind thanking the god.
- Greek temples were often in very healthy places; they had baths, and arenas for exercise, and people slept in abatons (open-air buildings). Perhaps this is why many got better — or maybe it was their **faith** that helped them. They were convinced that the gods would help them and this gave them the strength they needed to get well.

Ancient Rome (c. 200 BC–c. AD 500)

The Romans conquered Greece and took up many Greek ideas about medicine.

- They were more interested in the **prevention** of disease and built up vast **public health schemes** throughout their empire. No new ideas about the *causes* of disease appeared, but the Romans learned from experience that disease could spread in areas where there were swamps or marshes. They were careful to build new forts and towns well away from such areas.

- Most doctors in Rome were Greeks — often brought to Rome as prisoners of war. They were not generally popular and many Romans preferred to depend on the head of the household for medical treatment.
- There was one important development in the *treatment* of illness. **Galen**, a Greek doctor in Rome, developed treatments based on the **use of opposites**. He believed in the theory of four humours, but he developed it by treating patients with the opposite of their ailment. For example, for a cold he would prescribe a hot bath and pepper. Galen helped to keep other Hippocratic ideas going in Rome, besides becoming the greatest authority on human anatomy. His work, however, was based on the dissection of animals, as religious beliefs at the time made the dissection of humans impossible.
- As in ancient Greece, **supernatural ideas** continued alongside natural ideas. The Romans also believed in many gods and even built temples in honour of Asclepios.

Conclusion

Some significant progress in medicine was made in the ancient world:

- A new theory was developed based on natural explanations of disease.
- Medical knowledge was recorded.
- High standards were expected of doctors.
- There was greater understanding of cleanliness and exercise as means of staying healthy.
- Treatments based on natural substances, such as herbs, continued throughout this period.

However:

- Beliefs that gods and spirits could cause or cure disease continued to exist.
- It was impossible to make much progress towards under-standing the causes of disease because the technology needed to help doctors know about germs had not yet been developed.

Topic 1   Medicine in the ancient world

Use the information provided, your class notes and your textbook to answer the following questions.

1 What belief about the cause of disease existed in prehistoric times and continued throughout the period of the ancient world?

2 What explanation has been given for trephining as practised by prehistoric people?

3 Describe the new theory about disease which developed in ancient Egypt.

4 What treatments were based on this theory?

5 What remained the most common explanation of disease in ancient Egypt?

6 Describe the new theory about disease that was developed in ancient Greece.

7 What treatments linked to this theory would a Greek doctor recommend?

8 Where in ancient Greece would someone go to be cured by a god?

9 What did the ancient Greeks believe would happen at such a place?

1

2

3

4

5

6

7

8

9

Questions

10 How could we explain the fact that some people were 'cured' there?

10 _____
_____
_____
_____

11 Describe three ways in which the standard of work of Hippocratic doctors improved in ancient Greece.

11 _____
_____
_____

12 Give three reasons to explain why important new ideas developed during the period of ancient Greece.

12 _____
_____
_____
_____

13 The theory of the four humours was clearly wrong. Why, then, is it still considered to be important in the history of medicine?

13 _____
_____

14 What new idea about the cause of disease did the Romans develop and how did this affect where they built forts and towns?

14 _____
_____

15 What new form of treatment for illness was developed by Galen?

15 _____
_____
_____

16 Why did Galen's work on anatomy sometimes contain errors?

16 _____
_____

17 Select items from the following lists and write them in the appropriate space on the chart. Some will be used more than once.

Ideas about cause
Gods and spirits
New theory —
    blockages in body
Humours out of
    balance
New ideas — swamps
    and marshes
New theory — four
    humours out of
    balance

Treatments
Go to Asclepion
Rest — to get
    humours balanced
Bloodletting
Use of herbs
Go to medicine man
Trephining
New idea — use of
    opposites
Go to head of
    household
Pray to gods
Spells and magic
    potions
Remove blockages,
    e.g. by laxatives

Prevention
Public health schemes
Build towns, forts away
    from swamps
Keep fit
Take care over diet
Personal cleanliness —
    for good health
Charms
Cleanliness — for religious
    reasons
Nomadic way of life helped

Doctors
Mostly Greeks — not
    popular
Used Hippocratic
    methods, e.g. clinical
    observation
High standards of
    behaviour
Medicine men
Used mainly spells and
    potions
Medical ideas collected
    into books
Began to record treat-
    ments but mainly
    spells

17 Medicine in the ancient world: summary chart

Period	Ideas about cause	Treatments	Prevention	Doctors
Prehistoric times				
Ancient Egypt				
Ancient Greece				
Ancient Rome				

Questions

Source questions

18 Source A shows a trephined skull. What can you learn from this source about medicine in prehistoric times?

Source A

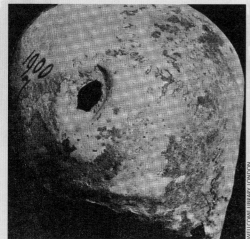

A skull from the Stone Age

19 Study Sources B and C. Source B says that Hippocrates taught that gods did not cause or cure disease. Source C shows that people still believed a god could cure disease. Does Source C mean that Source B is wrong? Explain your answer using Sources B and C and your own knowledge.

Source B

Hippocrates said that since the gods did not cause all diseases, doctors could work out how to cure people. Greek doctors began to observe their patients very carefully. They wrote down what they saw and worked out which humours were unbalanced — and what treatments were needed.

From *Medicine and Health through Time* by A. Moore, I. Dawson and I. Coulson, a textbook for schools published in 2002

Source C

Ambrosia of Athens became blind in one eye. When she went to the temple she dreamed the god stood beside her. He seemed to cut into her diseased eye and pour in medicine. When she woke in the morning she was cured.

An inscription found on a stone tablet near an Asclepion in ancient Greece

18

19

Extended writing

On separate paper, write a short essay in answer to the following question.

20 To what extent is it true to say that progress was made in the understanding and treatment of disease during the period of the ancient world? In your answer, use Sources A, B and C and your own knowledge.

20

Guidelines

A very good answer will include:

- references to Sources A, B and C, and additional knowledge not shown in the sources, to support your answer
- examples of progress, such as Hippocratic ideas and a natural theory of disease
- an explanation of factors that limited progress, such as religion and a lack of technology
- a conclusion that contains a reasoned judgement answering the question set

The early Middle Ages (c. AD 500–1100)

The centuries following the collapse of the Roman Empire are sometimes called the 'Dark Ages' because they were characterised by frequent wars and instability. This had important consequences for medicine, which saw a period of **regression** — that is, things got worse.

- Libraries were destroyed and many Greek and Roman medical texts were lost.
- The training of doctors ceased.
- The public health schemes of the Romans were largely destroyed (see Topic 5).

The later Middle Ages (1100–1500)

This was a more stable era and progress was made in some areas of medicine.

Explanations for disease

The most common explanation continued to be the Greek theory of the four humours. One new theory that developed and existed alongside this was based on the idea that people's health could be affected by the positions of the stars and planets.

Religion continued to be a powerful influence on beliefs, and disease was often seen as a punishment from God.

Treatments

These were usually based on the theory of the four humours. For example, bloodletting was regularly used both to maintain good health and to treat illness. The colour of a patient's urine became a common means of diagnosing illness and a **Zodiac Man chart** was often used to help a physician decide the best time for letting blood.

The continued use of herbal remedies provided some effective treatments.

The training of doctors

By the 1300s the Church had set up many universities, where the training of doctors was becoming well organised. In some places, such as Montpelier in France, it was sometimes possible to observe the dissection of the body of an executed criminal, although this was intended merely to help students learn the works of Galen. Questioning of Galen's work was not encouraged. The Church supported the study of Galen because he seemed to believe in one 'creator' — an idea that fitted in with Christian teaching that there was only one God.

Only wealthy people could afford to consult a trained doctor. Ordinary people tended to rely on local 'wise women' or monks for medical advice.

Surgery

The problems of pain, bleeding and infection continued to prevent significant progress in surgery. Only operations close to the surface of the body were successful.

Wars in the later Middle Ages led to greater skills in treating war wounds. **Wound Man** illustrations showed the war wounds that battle surgeons claimed to be able to treat. In Italy, for example, surgeons improved methods of removing arrows from wounds, and Hugh of Lucca showed how wine could help prevent infection. Some surgeons attempted to use sleep-inducing drugs like opium as an anaesthetic.

Some educated 'master surgeons' treated the rich, but the barber-surgeons, who did minor operations like bloodletting, tooth pulling and setting fractures (as well as haircuts and shaving), were more common.

The impact of religion on medicine in the Middle Ages

Influence of Islam

Islam was founded by Muhammad in Arabia in 622 and spread rapidly throughout the Middle East, Asia and North Africa in the Middle Ages.

In one way Islam hindered the development of medicine. Human dissections were forbidden and this held back the study of anatomy. However, Islam made three important contributions to medicine:

- **Development of hospitals.** The Islamic holy book — the Qur'an — taught that taking care of the sick and needy was a vital part of Muslim faith. Hospitals were therefore built in Baghdad and many other cities. The Christian (Catholic) Church also provided hospitals in the Middle Ages, but Islamic hospitals were better because they offered treatment as well as care, and doctors were always present. Hospitals were also provided for the mentally ill, who were treated as if they were ill — not possessed by evil spirits.

- **Preservation of ancient Greek and Roman medical texts.** Islamic scholars picked up and developed many of the ideas of ancient Greeks and Romans like Hippocrates and Galen. Baghdad became a centre for the translation of Greek manuscripts, which were studied by Arab medical students. Thus, these important works were preserved and could later be translated back into Latin for Western scholars.

- **Work of important individuals. Avicenna** (Ibn Sinna), a famous Arabic doctor and teacher, wrote a book called the *Canon of Medicine*, which covered all aspects of medicine known at this time. **Rhazes** (*c.* 852– *c.* 925), a Persian doctor, was the first person to describe accurately the difference between measles and smallpox, and he wrote over 150 books on medicine. **Ibn Al Nafis** in 1242 became the first person to realise that Galen's idea that blood 'flowed' around the body was wrong, but his work was not studied outside the Middle East. Consequently, Galen's error continued to be taught in medical schools for another 400 years.

Influence of the Christian Church

The Christian Church also had great influence on people's beliefs and lives. Church leaders had as much power as kings and queens. This power was used both to *help* and to *hinder* medical progress.

How the Church HELPED medicine

- The Church taught that people had a duty to help care for the sick, and monks gave free medical advice and treatment.
- Many hospitals were set up by the Church, especially between AD 1000 and 1399. Most were small, for about 12 patients.
- Special hospitals for **lepers** were set up by the Church — about 19,000 existed by the year 1225.
- The Church established universities in the 1300s where doctors could be trained. Dissections were sometimes allowed, to show Galen's ideas.

How the Church HINDERED medicine

- The Church taught people not to question old ways and that prayer was more likely to bring about cures than doctors.
- Monks and nuns ran the hospitals and aimed only to keep patients comfortable and to save their souls. Doctors were rarely present.
- The Church taught that mentally ill people were being punished by God and were possessed by devils or evil spirits.
- The Church discouraged dissection in general and any challenges to Galen's ideas. This held back the study of **anatomy**.

In medieval Europe, people believed that illness could be cured by saints. Praying to a particular saint — or going on a **pilgrimage** to the saint's tomb or shrine — might result in a cure. Many pilgrims made offerings to the saint when they reached the shrine. The churches and cathedrals that housed important shrines became the richest in the land. It was claimed that many 'cures' happened at these shrines, but these could have been natural recoveries, or the result of strong faith or a change of air and diet.

By the end of the Middle Ages (*c.* 1500), the Catholic Church was becoming far less powerful.
- The invention of the printing press in the fifteenth century meant that more and more people could read the Bible and they were beginning to question some teachings of the Church.
- The Reformation had begun and many Christian groups were beginning to break away from the Catholic Church.

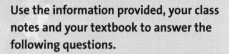

Use the information provided, your class notes and your textbook to answer the following questions.

1 By what other name is the period of the early Middle Ages known?

2 Describe two ways in which medicine declined during that period.

3 Describe a new explanation for disease that developed during the Middle Ages.

4 Describe one old explanation for disease that continued in this period.

5 In what ways did the training of doctors improve in the Middle Ages?

6 In what way was this training limited?

7 Why would a doctor or barber-surgeon use a Zodiac Man chart?

8 What three problems prevented major improvement in surgery?

9 What did Wound Man pictures show?

10 What sort of work did barber-surgeons do?

11 Describe any two ways in which Islamic peoples helped medicine to progress.

1
2
3
4
5
6
7
8
9
10
11

Questions

12 Describe any two ways in which the Christian Church helped medicine to progress.

13 Describe one way in which both the Islamic and Christian religions hindered medical progress.

14 What different attitudes towards mental illness did the Islamic and Christian faiths have?

15 Describe one important difference between a Christian hospital and an Islamic hospital.

16 How could we explain why pilgrims were sometimes cured after visiting a shrine?

17 How might a medieval priest have explained why a sick person was *not* cured after visiting a shrine?

18 Why did the Church have less influence over people's lives by the end of the fifteenth century?

12

13

14

15

16

17

18

19 Complete the summary chart by writing your own notes in the blank spaces.

19 Medicine in the Middle Ages: summary chart

Area of medicine	Old belief/ problem that continued	New belief/development in later Middle Ages	A sign of progress or not? Why?
Explanations for disease			
Treating disease			
Training doctors			
Surgery			

Questions

Source questions

20 What can you learn from Source A about the importance of religion in the later Middle Ages? Explain your answer using the source and your own knowledge.

Source A

A fifteenth-century exorcism. The Latin caption says: 'A bishop drives out evil spirits'

WELLCOME LIBRARY, LONDON

21 How far does Source B show that progress in medicine had occurred by the end of the Middle Ages? Explain your answer using the source and your own knowledge.

Source B

A dissection scene from 1482

WELLCOME LIBRARY, LONDON

20

_____

_____

_____

_____

_____

_____

_____

_____

_____

_____

_____

21

_____

_____

_____

_____

_____

_____

_____

_____

_____

_____

_____

_____

_____

_____

_____

_____

Extended writing

On separate paper, write your answers to the following two questions.

22 'Religion did far more to hinder medical progress in the Middle Ages than it did to help it.' Using Sources A and B above and your own knowledge, explain why you agree or disagree with this interpretation.

22

Guidelines

A very good answer will include:

- references to Sources A and B, and additional knowledge not shown in the sources, to support your answer
- examples of the ways in which religion both hindered and helped medical progress — drawn from both the Islamic and Christian faiths
- a clear conclusion where a supported judgement is made in answer to the question set

23 The medical ideas of the ancient Greeks had a lot of influence on medieval doctors. Did this do more to help them or hinder them? Explain your answer.

23 You could include the following in your answer and other information of your own:

- In the Hippocratic Oath, doctors promised to maintain very high standards of behaviour towards their patients.
- Medical students in the Middle Ages studied Galen.
- Treatments in the Middle Ages were often based on the theory of the four humours.

A new age

This was an era very different in character from the Middle Ages. It saw a 'rebirth' of interest in the ancient civilisations of Greece and Rome — especially in their art and architecture, but also in the writings of people like Hippocrates and Galen. Voyages of exploration to the 'new' world of the Americas made people feel they were living in an exciting new age and they were more confident about questioning and challenging old ideas and old ways. This helped bring change and progress to some areas of medicine.

Influences on the progress of medicine

The following factors also played an important part in the development of medicine during this period:

- **New technology.** The printing press had been invented in 1454 (by Johannes Gutenberg). This meant that books could be printed, so new ideas spread more quickly.
- **The Church was less powerful.** Now that more people could read the Bible for themselves, they were more inclined to question some of the teachings of the Church. In northern Europe, the Reformation meant that new Protestant churches were replacing Catholic ones. It became easier for people to do dissections even though the Church was still against it.
- **New styles of art.** These began in Italy in the middle of the fifteenth century and gradually spread across Europe. This meant that more realistic and accurate pictures of dissections could be made and printed in books.
- **Brilliant individuals**, such as Vesalius and Harvey. **Paracelsus**, a Swiss scientist, was less influential but he was one of the first to challenge the old ideas. He rejected the theory of the four humours and in 1527 publicly burned Galen's books.

Vesalius and anatomy

In the Middle Ages, students had learned anatomy by studying the works of Galen. In some medical schools, such as at Montpelier in France, it had sometimes been possible to observe a human dissection. The professor read extracts from Galen while an assistant dissected the corpse, but there was little discussion.

Andreas Vesalius became a professor of anatomy in the Italian university of Padua in 1537. He studied the works of Galen closely and admired him greatly. However, when Vesalius began to do dissections himself, he started to realise that sometimes there were errors in Galen's work. For example, Galen had said the human jaw consisted of two bones, but Vesalius saw that there was only one. At first, Vesalius was heavily criticised by other teachers of anatomy. How could Galen be wrong when his work had been studied for over 1,000 years?

Vesalius proved he was right by doing dissections in public and inviting students to come close and see what he could see. In 1543 he published all he had learned in his book, *The Fabric of the Human Body*. Thanks to the printing press, this book was soon being studied in every medical school in Europe. Thanks to the new styles in art, the book also contained accurate woodcuts and drawings of Vesalius's dissections so that others could see what he had found.

Impact of Vesalius's work

His main achievements were to show that:
- The work of Galen could no longer be accepted without question.
- If people really wanted to learn more about human anatomy, they had to do dissections themselves and not just study books or watch a demonstration.

As a result of Vesalius's work, the teaching of anatomy had been changed in an important way. His work did not, however, bring doctors any closer to understanding the true causes of disease, and treatments continued to be based on old theories like that of the four humours.

Harvey and the circulation of blood

Most scientists still believed Galen's theory that blood was made in the liver and then flowed around the body, passing from one side of the heart to the other through tiny holes in the septum (the wall which separates the left ventricle from the right ventricle), until gradually being used up. The liver kept on making more.

When **William Harvey** (1578–1657), an English doctor and lecturer in anatomy, published his main work in 1628, he was greatly criticised by some scientists who would not accept that Galen might be wrong. Harvey found that:
- Blood circulated and moved in one direction, leaving the heart through arteries and returning via veins.
- The heart was a pump, driving the blood around the body.

What helped Harvey make his discoveries?

- Harvey was living in a more scientific age, so he tested his theories and proved them correct by **experiments**. Others could then repeat these and see that he was right. He dissected live cold-blooded animals whose hearts beat slowly, so that he could observe the movement of muscles in the heart.
- Vesalius had already shown that Galen was wrong in some ways. This made it easier for Harvey to convince some people that Galen might be wrong about the liver making blood.
- Harvey was a student at Padua for a short time (1600–02) and was taught by Fabricius, a professor of anatomy who had shown that valves were present in veins, making blood flow one way.
- Harvey lived at a time when water pumps were used, and seeing these might have helped him to develop his theory.

Was Harvey's work a turning point?

Harvey's work cannot really be considered a turning point because it did not lead to any rapid change:
- Bloodletting continued for many years after his death.
- Doctors could not use this new knowledge for the more effective treatment of patients. It did not help them to understand the causes of disease either.
- Blood transfusions were attempted, but they were not successful because knowledge of different blood groups still did not exist.

However, his work was important in the long term:

- Other scientists built on his knowledge and learned more about the tiny capillaries that allow blood to pass from the arteries to the veins — and later about how the blood carries oxygen around the body. Harvey was convinced that capillaries existed, but he could not see them because microscopes had not yet been invented.
- Harvey made a big contribution to the development of **scientific method**. Others saw how he proved his theories correct by experiments and they copied his method.

The death of Charles II

The death of Charles II in 1685 helps show the limits of medical knowledge by the end of this period. The king fell ill on the evening of 2 February 1685. He felt 'some unusual disturbance in his brain, soon followed by loss of speech and convulsions'.

Sir Charles Scarburgh, one of the king's physicians, made a detailed account of the treatments planned and given to Charles II in his final days by 12 of the best doctors in the land. These treatments included:

- bloodletting at regular intervals
- medicine to make him vomit in order to 'free his stomach of all impurities'
- an enema — an injection of liquid into the rectum to empty his bowels
- shaving his hair and applying blistering agents to his head
- pills 'to drain away the humours'
- medicine containing on one occasion spirit of human skull and on another Oriental Bezoar stone — taken from the stomach of a goat

Do you think these treatments helped or worsened the king's health?

Conclusion

The Renaissance was a more scientific age than previous eras, but despite the achievements of Vesalius and Harvey, doctors were still no closer to understanding the true cause of diseases or to finding effective cures for them.

Topic 3

Medicine during the Renaissance: c. 1500–1700

Use the information provided, your class notes and your textbook to answer the following questions.

1 Complete the chart by arranging the following events in chronological order and putting the correct dates beside them.
- King Charles II died
- Harvey's work on the circulation of blood was published
- Vesalius published *The Fabric of the Human Body*
- Paracelsus publicly burned the works of Galen

2 When, roughly, was the period of history called the Renaissance?

3 How was anatomy taught before Vesalius?

4 What did Vesalius discover?

5 How was anatomy taught after Vesalius?

1 Medicine during the Renaissance: timeline of events

Date	Event

2

3

4

5

Questions

6 Explain how each of these factors helped
Vesalius bring about this change in the
study of anatomy:
a new technology
b the reduced power of the Church
c the development of new styles of art
d living at the time of the Renaissance

6a

b

c

d

7 What beliefs about blood were accepted
before Harvey?

7

8 What did Harvey discover?

8

9 Write brief notes on the diagram to explain four factors that helped Harvey make his discoveries.

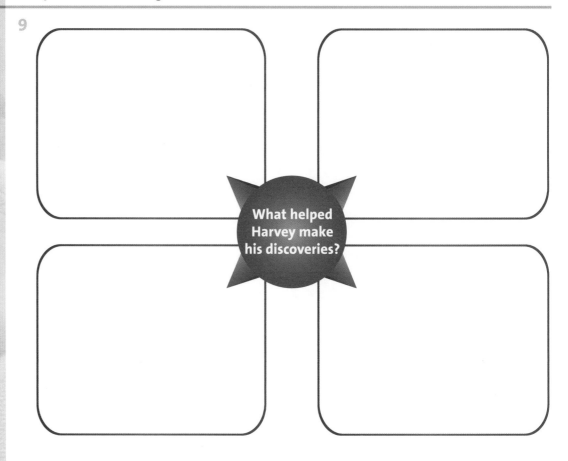

What helped Harvey make his discoveries?

Questions

10 New ideas in medicine were often opposed by others when they were made public. Explain why the ideas of these individuals were attacked:
   a Vesalius
   b Harvey

10a
_____
_____
_____
_____

b
_____
_____
_____
_____

11 The phrase 'turning point' is sometimes used to describe a discovery that set an area of medicine off in an important new direction. To what extent can the work of these individuals be described as 'turning points' in the history of medicine?
   a Vesalius
   b Harvey

11a
_____
_____
_____
_____
_____

b
_____
_____
_____
_____
_____

Source A

WELLCOME LIBRARY, LONDON

Andreas Vesalius, from The Fabric of the Human Body, *1543*

Source B

Harvey's explanation that blood circulated around the body, pumped by the heart, was published first in Germany after a deliberate delay. This is because he thought he would be laughed at or persecuted. 'I dread that all men will turn against me', he wrote. For some time Harvey was regarded as 'crackbrained' and many patients refused to be treated by him.

From *The Early Modern Age 1400–1714* by L. Snellgrove, a general history textbook for schools published in 1972

Source C

The period of the Renaissance saw important advances in medicine. The work of Harvey, for example, meant great progress was made in understanding how the human body worked. He helped put the study of anatomy on a more scientific footing.

Adapted from *Medicine through Time* by B. Rees and P. Shuter, a history textbook for schools published in 1996

Source questions

12 How does Source A help you to understand how Vesalius changed the study of anatomy? Explain your answer using the source.

13 Study Sources B and C. In what ways do Sources B and C differ in their portrayal of Harvey's role in the development of anatomy? In your answer, use Sources B and C and your own knowledge.

12

13

Questions

Extended writing

On separate paper, write your answers to these two questions.

14 To what extent was the progress made in medicine during the Renaissance due solely to the brilliance of individual people? In your answer, make use of Sources A, B and C and your own knowledge.

14

Guidelines

A very good answer will include:

- references to Sources A, B and C and additional knowledge not in the sources
- explanations of how individual brilliance (Vesalius and Harvey) brought progress
- explanations of how other factors (for example, new styles in art, the decline in the power of the Church and the use of mechanical pumps) also helped Vesalius and Harvey
- a reasoned conclusion

15 Did the training of doctors improve more in the Middle Ages or in the Renaissance (c. 1500–1700)? Explain your answer.

15 You could include the following in your answer or any other information of your own:

- Students of medicine were able to observe dissections in the Middle Ages.
- Vesalius did his own dissections.
- Charles II was treated by the best doctors in the country in 1685.

The development of vaccinations

Today we are protected from many dangerous diseases through **vaccination**. The first ever vaccine was discovered by **Edward Jenner**, a country doctor in Gloucestershire. In 1798 he published research which showed that vaccination with a mild disease, cowpox, protected people from **smallpox**. Smallpox had been a killer disease for centuries. Sufferers who did not die were often left with terrible scars for the rest of their lives.

The Chinese had already discovered that someone who had a mild form of the disease never got the serious form. They started the practice of **inoculation**. This meant taking pus from a scab on a person with the mild form and rubbing it into a scratch on the arm of a healthy person.

Lady Mary Wortley Montague, who learned about inoculation in Turkey, brought the idea to England in 1721 and had her own son inoculated. Inoculation became popular among the wealthier classes, but poorer people could not afford to have it done.

Some doctors made a great deal of money by inoculating patients. Inoculation significantly reduced the number of people who died from smallpox in the 1700s, but it was risky. Sometimes people did develop the serious form of smallpox and died. In 1783 the son of George III died this way.

In country areas like Gloucestershire, where Jenner lived, other people had noticed that if you caught cowpox, you never went on to catch smallpox. However, it was Jenner in 1796 who first began to experiment in a systematic way with cowpox. A young boy called James Phipps was successfully vaccinated with pus taken from a milkmaid who had cowpox. Jenner published his findings in 1798 after 2 years of trials with cowpox. He called his discovery 'vaccination' after the Latin word *vacca*, meaning 'cow'.

Opposition

Jenner's discovery was not welcomed by everyone:
- Some London doctors did not believe that an unknown country doctor could make such an important discovery; others feared an end to their profitable inoculation businesses.
- Some doctors were less careful than Jenner and sometimes vaccinated with smallpox by mistake instead of cowpox.
- The Anti-Vaccine Society suggested that using cowpox might turn you into an animal.
- The main reason why some people would not accept Jenner's vaccine was that neither Jenner nor anyone else could explain how or why it worked. Jenner did not even know that a germ caused smallpox. The **germ theory** of disease had not yet been discovered.

Despite this, many people did welcome Jenner's discovery:
- Parliament awarded him a grant of £30,000 in 1802 to open a vaccination clinic in London.
- Many doctors from across Britain began to use his method of vaccination.
- In 1802 Thomas Jefferson, the US president, sent Jenner a letter thanking him for his work.
- In 1805 the French emperor, Napoleon, had his army vaccinated.

Why was vaccination developed at this time?

Several factors helped to bring about the medical development of vaccination at this particular time:

- Inoculations to give protection from smallpox were already common, so this may have given Jenner the idea for his trial vaccinations.
- Living in a country area made Jenner aware that people who had cowpox never got smallpox.
- It was more common by the 1790s for people to do experiments in order to test theories.
- Jenner himself was a trained doctor and a member of the Royal Society (for scientific research).
- Jenner was an outstanding individual. He observed something interesting and investigated it further.

How important was Jenner's discovery in the history of medicine?

Vaccination was a very important discovery in terms of saving lives because:

- It protected millions of people from smallpox and eventually meant that the disease disappeared from the world.
- The French chemist Louis Pasteur read about Jenner's work and later produced other vaccines (see below).

However, it did not lead to the immediate development of other vaccines. Jenner could not explain *how* or *why* it worked, so no one could copy his methods. It was not until Pasteur's discovery 80 years later that further progress with vaccines was possible — Pasteur was able to explain how vaccines work.

Government involvement was needed to bring smallpox completely under control. Until 1852 vaccination was voluntary and the poor often could not afford it. After 1852, vaccination was meant to be compulsory, but this was not strictly enforced. It was only after 1872, when the government ensured that everyone was vaccinated, that smallpox began to disappear (see Table 1). Some people objected to compulsory vaccination. They said it was wrong for the government to interfere in health matters and force people to be vaccinated. Discovery of the vaccine did not then, in itself, end smallpox.

Table 1 Smallpox fatalities, 1850–1930

Year	Deaths from smallpox per million of the population
1850	210
1870	300
1890	10
1910	10
1930	0

Pasteur and the second vaccine, 1880

Louis Pasteur had always been interested in Jenner's work. In 1878 he learned that a sheep which recovered from the disease **anthrax** could not catch it again.

Using **Robert Koch**'s technique of growing cultures of germs (see below), Pasteur was also investigating, with funding from the French government, another animal disease — **chicken cholera**.

In 1880 Pasteur's assistant injected some chickens by chance with an old culture of germs. When they did not die, Pasteur's skill and training led him to investigate further by setting up an experiment. He discovered that injection with a weak culture of germs enabled the body to develop **immunity** (protection) against stronger germs. As a tribute to Jenner, Pasteur called this 'vaccination'. He had discovered how vaccines worked and quickly developed vaccines for anthrax (1881) and rabies (1884).

Other scientists now knew how to research and make vaccines for other diseases. Early in the twentieth century, vaccines were developed for tuberculosis (in 1906 by **Albert Calmette** and **Camille Guérin**) and diphtheria (in 1913 by **Emil Behring** who had discovered a cure for diptheria earlier, in 1890). Today, we are protected from a variety of infectious diseases such as whooping cough and German measles by vaccinations given in childhood.

The germ theory of disease

The first microscopes were developed in the latter part of the 1600s. However, for some time the germs, which could now be seen, were thought to appear as a result of decay. This was called the theory of spontaneous generation. It was not until the 1860s that Louis Pasteur was able, using carefully conducted experiments and more highly developed microscopes, to prove that these microorganisms caused things to decay.

Pasteur only became involved in this field when local brewers asked him to investigate why their alcohol sometimes went bad during the brewing process. He showed that microorganisms could be killed through heating (**pasteurisation**) and he believed that they almost certainly caused disease.

Finally, in the 1870s, the German scientist Robert Koch was able to identify the particular microbes that caused particular diseases, and thus the **germ theory** (the idea that germs caused disease) was established. This is why we tend to give both Pasteur and Koch credit for this important breakthrough.

Koch also developed new ways of studying germs by showing how they could be:
- stained by using chemical dyes
- photographed through a microscope
- grown in cultures on agar jelly

Although they were working in similar fields, Pasteur and Koch never worked together. In fact, national rivalry between the Frenchman and the German may have spurred them on in their work. (In 1870, France fought and lost a war against Prussia and, as a result, lost the region of Alsace-Lorraine to the new Germany that was created in 1871.)

Individual brilliance obviously played a large part in their success, but both men benefited from government help that funded much of their research as well as from the development of new technology — most importantly, more powerful microscopes.

The germ theory was probably the most important turning point in the whole history of medicine. It led to major developments in surgery in the late 1860s and in public health in the mid-1870s (see Topics 6 and 7). It meant that the true cause of disease was finally understood. Scientists could now look for ways of both curing and preventing infectious diseases.

The hunt was on for chemical substances that would destroy germs in patients without harming them. The first of these so-called **magic bullets** was discovered in 1909 by a team led by **Paul Ehrlich**. This was **Salvarsan 606** and it cured syphilis.

The story of penicillin

The first **antibiotic** was discovered, partly by chance, by **Alexander Fleming** in 1928 when he noticed that a mould was killing staphy-lococci germs in a culture that he had been growing in a dish. Fleming identified the mould as **penicillin**. However, Fleming lacked the money and facilities to develop his work. In 1938, **Howard Florey** and **Ernst Chain** developed the study of penicillin further, showing through research and experiments that it was capable of killing a variety of germs. However, although the resources at their disposal were far greater than Fleming's, they were unable to produce penicillin in large enough quantities to make it a usable drug.

The Second World War now played a significant part in the story of penicillin. With soldiers and civilians dying from infected wounds, there was an urgent need for a new wonder drug. In 1942 the US government gave the large drug companies in the USA $75 million for the equipment needed to start mass producing penicillin and by 1944 supplies were available for Allied casualties in Europe. In 1945, Fleming, Florey and Chain were jointly awarded the Nobel Prize for the development of penicillin. Fleming, however, became more famous than the other two since he enjoyed the publicity much more than they did and gave many more interviews to the media. Since then, antibiotics such as streptomycin, tetracyclin and mitomycin have been developed.

Fighting disease today

The battle against infectious diseases has largely been won, although some problems remain:
- The causes of some non-infectious diseases, such as cancer, are still not fully understood.
- Some 'super bugs' have emerged in recent years which are resistant to modern drugs.
- No cures exist for viruses like **HIV**, which eventually causes AIDS.

In 1967 an international body, the **World Health Organization** (WHO), started a campaign to wipe out smallpox. This was so successful that since 1980 there have been no cases of smallpox anywhere in the world. In 1987 the WHO began a worldwide programme designed to fight the spread of AIDS.

Thanks to the work of an Englishman, **Francis Crick**, an American, **James Watson**, and a New Zealander, **Maurice Wilkins**, our knowledge of the structure of **DNA** has increased greatly since the 1950s. This has created the possibility that knowledge of **genetics** may be used to cure or eliminate hereditary diseases.

Use the information provided, your class notes and your textbook to answer the following questions.

1 Complete the chart by listing the following events in the correct chronological order and including their dates.
- Penicillin was first seen to be capable of killing germs
- No cases of smallpox have been reported since this time
- The second vaccine was developed to protect chickens from chicken cholera
- Pasteur showed that microorganisms caused things to decay
- The first chemical cure — Salvarsan 606 — was discovered
- Work on the first ever vaccine — for smallpox — was published
- A cure for diphtheria was discovered
- A vaccine for tuberculosis was discovered

2 How did people try to protect themselves from smallpox before a vaccine was developed?

3 How successful was this method of inoculation?

1 The battle against infectious disease: timeline of events

Date	Event

2 _____

_____

3 _____

_____

_____

Questions

4 Give two reasons to explain why some people opposed the use of Jenner's vaccine.

4

5 Study Table 1 on page 29.
   a How do you explain the fact that so many people were still dying of smallpox more than 70 years after Jenner's vaccine was developed?
   b What brought about the improvement after the 1870s?

5a

b

6 Why didn't Jenner's vaccine lead quickly to the development of other vaccines?

6

7 What factors helped to bring about the development of the first ever vaccine in the 1790s?

7

8 Explain how each of the following helped to bring about the further development of vaccines in 1880:

a knowledge of Jenner's work

b money

c chance

d individual brilliance

8a

b

c

d

9 Of the four factors listed in question 8, which one would you say was the most important? Explain your answer.

9

10 Describe Louis Pasteur's contribution to our understanding of germs. In your answer refer to:
- what people believed about germs before Pasteur
- what Pasteur proved

10

11 What techniques for studying germs were developed by Robert Koch?

11

Questions

12 Who was more important in the development of the germ theory of disease, Pasteur or Koch? Explain your answer.

13 Why was the germ theory of disease an important breakthrough in the history of medicine?

14 Explain how each of the following contributed to the development of penicillin:
a the Second World War
b government involvement
c industry
d chance
e brilliant individuals

15 Which of the five factors listed in question 14 was most important in the successful development of penicillin? Explain your answer fully.

12

13

14a

b

c

d

e

15

16 Complete the chart by writing in the spaces provided the correct names from the following list:

- Albert Calmette and Camille Guérin
- Robert Koch
- Alexander Fleming
- Edward Jenner
- Francis Watson, James Crick and Maurice Wilkins
- Howard Florey and Ernst Chain
- Louis Pasteur
- Paul Ehrlich
- Emil Behring
- Lady Mary Wortley Montague

16 Individuals responsible for medical developments

Medical development	Individual(s) responsible
First brought the idea of inoculations against smallpox to England	
Developed the first ever vaccine — for smallpox	
Showed how vaccines worked and that germs caused things to decay	
Identified germs causing particular diseases and developed techniques for studying them	
Developed both a cure and a vaccine for diphtheria	
Developed a vaccine for tuberculosis	
Discovered the first chemical compound that could cure — Salvarsan 606	
Discovered penicillin but was unable to develop it into a usable medicine	
Continued research on penicillin and showed its potential for killing many germs	
Discovered the structure of DNA which may lead to genetic cures for disease one day	

Questions

Source questions

17 How useful is Source A in helping us to understand how people felt at that time about Jenner's vaccine? Explain your answer using the source and your own knowledge.

Source A

The COW-POCK — or — the Wonderful Effects of the New Inoculation! — Vide. the Publications of ỹ Anti-Vaccine Society.

A cartoon from 1802 produced by the Anti-Vaccine Society

WELLCOME LIBRARY, LONDON

Source B

Sir,

In the leading article on penicillin yesterday, you refrained from giving the credit for penicillin to any one person. It should be given to Professor Alexander Fleming of this research laboratory. For he is the discoverer of penicillin and was the author also of the original suggestion that the substance might prove to have important applications in medicine.

I am, Sir, yours faithfully,

Almroth Wright,

Inoculation Department, St Mary's Hospital

A letter to the editor of *The Times*, 28 August 1942. Almroth Wright was head of the department in which Fleming worked

Source C

Fleming's role in the story of penicillin generally has been exaggerated. He was hampered by his inability to purify the substance and by his lack of chemical knowledge...There is evidence that he was not convinced that the problem of isolating and purifying the active part of penicillium could be overcome.

From *Disease and its Control* by Robert P. Hudson, published in 1983

18 Compare Sources B and C. Using these sources and your own knowledge, explain why these interpretations of Alexander Fleming's work are so different.

18

_____

_____

_____

_____

_____

_____

_____

_____

_____

_____

_____

_____

Extended writing

On separate paper, write a short essay in answer to the following question.

19 'The discovery of penicillin makes Sir Alexander Fleming the most important individual in medicine in the twentieth century.' Do you agree or disagree with this statement? Explain your answer using Sources B and C and your own knowledge.

19

Guidelines

A very good answer will include:

- references to Sources B and C and additional knowledge not in these sources
- an explanation of why Fleming's discovery was very important and understanding that other people and other factors played an important part in the development of penicillin
- knowledge about other individuals who made important discoveries in the twentieth century
- a conclusion that attempts to compare the importance of Fleming with the work of other individuals, and that expresses an opinion supported by sound reasoning

Public health in Roman Britain

The Romans conquered most of Britain in AD 43. They brought their usual health facilities to Britain, so a Roman town in Britain would have had:

- **public baths** (the most famous of these was at Bath)
- a system for bringing **fresh water** into towns, using clay pipes coated with concrete
- **public toilets** and **sewerage systems**

Bathhouses and **hospitals** were also found in military centres — for example, at Housesteads on Hadrian's Wall.

The Romans attached considerable importance to public health because:

- They had learned by experience that providing clean water and sewerage systems helped to prevent illness.
- They were a military power, so keeping their army healthy was very important.
- Bringing high standards to the countries they conquered helped to win over the loyalty of the people who lived in them to the Roman Empire.

As Britain was on the northern edge of the Roman Empire, it is likely that standards were not as high there as in towns closer to Rome itself. For example, only main towns like **York** and **Lincoln** had underground sewerage systems. In other, less important towns, open sewers were used and therefore unpleasant smells would have been common.

Water supplies went mainly to the bathhouses, so most people still had to get water from wells and streams. Similarly, few homes would have had indoor toilets, so most people used pots and emptied the contents into the streets or open sewers.

The Romans began to withdraw from Britain during the fifth century AD. The people who followed them, mostly Angles and Saxons, had neither the technical skills nor the interest to maintain the Roman systems of public health. Town life in Britain declined and with it went the Roman water and drainage systems.

Public health in the later Middle Ages, c. 1100–1500

By about 1100 town life had recovered, although clean water and sanitation played little part in the lives of most townspeople.

Rubbish was left in the streets and pollution of water supplies was a big problem. **Open streams** were used for washing clothes, but butchers would often dump the entrails of animals in them. Many people preferred to buy from water sellers who came around the streets.

Standards were lower than in the days of the Romans for three main reasons:

- The Romans had an efficient tax-collecting system and so had the money to meet the cost of providing public health measures. England in the Middle Ages lacked this kind of finance.

- Rome had a strong central government under the leadership of the emperor, and an efficient and well-organised civil service to ensure that the orders of the emperor were carried out. In medieval England, kings and queens could issue orders, but there was no effective civil service to make sure that things happened across the country.
- Most important of all, the Romans believed in public health systems as the best way of preventing disease. This belief was not common among those who governed England during the Middle Ages.

Attempts to maintain good standards of public health

It would be wrong to assume that no one cared about cleanliness or hygiene. Ordinary people would have done their best, while the wealthy could ensure that their houses had an indoor toilet on the ground floor, which would drain away into a **cesspit** somewhere in the garden. Wealthy people frequently gave money to the Church and this ensured that standards of cleanliness were higher in church buildings than in other places in Medieval England. Monasteries were often situated deliberately in river valleys so that fresh water could be taken directly from streams or nearby springs. In larger buildings, such as Canterbury Cathedral, water was piped to different areas to supply the kitchen and 'lavers' (wash rooms). Communal lavatories were placed in buildings called 'necessaria' or 'necessary houses', which were situated over the downstream end so that waste could be carried away.

Town councils or **town corporations** also sometimes tried to improve cleanliness and hygiene. For example, some provided public toilets (or latrines), employed **rakiers** to go around cleaning out cesspits and picking up rubbish, and passed by-laws to stop tradespeople like butchers dumping rubbish in the streets.

Richard ('Dick') Whittington, who was Mayor of London three times between 1397 and 1419, left money in his will for several public buildings, including a large public lavatory in London built next to the River Thames.

Plagues and epidemics

Poor standards of public health and disease tend to go hand in hand. In 1348 the plague known as the **Black Death** reached England. Over the next 2 years it killed around one third to one half of the population.

Explanations for the Black Death

It was impossible for people living at that time to understand the true cause of plague — or any other disease. The microscope had not been invented, so the existence of germs was still unknown.

These are some of the explanations put forward at the time:
- God had sent this disease to punish people for their sins.
- There were invisible poisons or **miasmas** in the air.
- There was an imbalance of the four humours in people's bodies.
- It was contagious. You caught the plague by touching the bodies or clothing of victims.

- The planets were in a particular position.
- Jews were poisoning streams and wells.

Attempts to stop the spread of the Black Death

A number of actions were taken to try to stop the plague spreading:
- Sweet-smelling things were burned in order to clean or purify the air of poisonous miasmas.
- People were encouraged to avoid crowding together, to keep away from plague victims and to avoid the 'stinks' of fields, streets and stagnant water.
- In 1349, Edward III ordered the Lord Mayor of London to clean up the streets to stop the smells and infected air that (he thought) were poisoning people.
- A religious group called **flagellants** travelled around Europe from town to town, whipping themselves and each other in the hope that God would forgive people for the sins of the world and stop the plague.
- In one part of Italy, the republic of Ragusa, sailors were made to leave ships at a special place away from the city. Anyone suspected of being in contact with the plague had to spend a **quarantenaria** (a period of 40 days) there before being allowed into the city. This is where our word 'quarantine' comes from.
- In parts of central Europe, many Jews were burned to death.

The Great Plague, 1665

Less serious outbreaks of plague continued to occur from time to time, most notably the **Great Plague** of 1665 that killed around 100,000 people in London alone.

The causes of disease were still not understood at this time:
- Some people thought the plague was contagious — spread by touch from person to person.
- Other people said it was the result of 'bad air'.
- It was also believed that the large number of stray dogs in the city were spreading the disease.

The Lord Mayor and aldermen of London did take action to try to contain the plague:
- Examiners and searchers identified houses where there was an infection.
- Infected houses were marked with a large cross and the words 'Lord have mercy on us'. These houses were shut up for a month and watchmen stood guard to ensure no one went in or out.
- The dead were collected and buried at night in deep graves.
- People were ordered to keep their streets clean and no animals were to be kept in the city. Stray dogs were killed.

The 1665 epidemic proved to be the last major outbreak of plague in Britain. However, standards of public health in towns and cities remained low and were to grow worse in the late eighteenth century as the Industrial Revolution got underway.

Use the information provided, your class notes and your textbook to answer the following questions.

1 Give three public health features that you would have found in a town in Roman Britain.

2 Were standards of public health high in all towns in Roman Britain? Explain your answer.

3 Why did standards of public health in Britain get worse after AD 500?

4 What sort of public health problems existed in English towns during the later Middle Ages?

5 Describe two steps taken by some town corporations to improve hygiene.

6 Give three reasons to explain why standards of public health were lower in the Middle Ages than in Roman Britain.

7 a State two beliefs about the causes of the Black Death that were based on natural explanations for disease.
  b State two beliefs that were **not** based on natural explanations.

1

2

3

4

5

6

7a

b

8 a Describe any two steps taken at the time which may have helped to stop the Black Death spreading.
  b Describe any two steps taken at the time which would definitely not have stopped the Black Death spreading.

8a
_____
_____
_____
_____

b
_____
_____
_____
_____

9 Describe any three steps taken in London in 1665 to try to stop the Great Plague from spreading.

9
_____
_____
_____
_____
_____
_____
_____
_____

Extended writing

On separate paper, write a short essay in answer to the following question.

10 'Governments in the past completely failed to maintain good standards of public health.' Do you think this was true of the period from Roman Britain to the end of the seventeenth century?

10 You could include the following in your answer and any other information of your own:

- The Romans built public baths in the city of Bath.
- In 1349 Edward III ordered the Lord Mayor of London to clean up the streets.
- In 1665 about 100,000 people in London died of plague.

The situation in 1800

At the beginning of the nineteenth century, living conditions in British towns and cities were terrible:

- Rubbish was dumped in the streets.
- There were no proper systems of water supply, sewerage or drainage.
- Disease was common and life expectancy was low.

There were four main reasons for these poor conditions:

- The **Industrial Revolution** had led to a very rapid growth of towns around the new factories.
- There were no regulations controlling the **building of houses**. Homes for workers were built cheaply, crowded together and lacking in proper provision of water and sewers.
- **Ignorance** — the connection between filthy living conditions and disease was still not understood.
- Governments at both national and local level believed in the policy of **laissez faire** — that governments should not get involved in the private lives of individuals, and people should be left to sort out their own affairs.

Edwin Chadwick

In the 1830s and 1840s, two factors led to some people demanding a change to laissez faire:

- the first terrible **cholera epidemic** of 1833, which affected both rich and poor
- the work of **Edwin Chadwick**, a civil servant and social reformer

Chadwick became convinced that sickness was a main cause of poverty and that it could be reduced if all towns were forced to set up boards of health. These boards of health would organise the building of proper water supply and sewerage systems. This would be paid for out of the local rates (a local tax like our council tax).

Chadwick published his ideas in a *Report on the Sanitary Conditions of the Labouring Classes* (1842).

Public Health Act, 1848

Mainly because of Chadwick's report, the **Public Health Act (1848)** was passed. As a result of this:

- A central board of health was set up in London for 5 years. Chadwick was a leading member.
- All towns could set up a local board of health if 10% of ratepayers agreed, but it was *not compulsory* to do so.

Chadwick tried to pressure more councils into taking action and made many enemies in the process. *The Times* newspaper accused Chadwick of 'bullying' people into being clean. Local businessmen were often reluctant to support health reforms because they would have to pay higher rates. Belief in laissez faire was also still strong.

Eventually, in 1854, Chadwick's enemies persuaded the government to sack him and the central board of health was abolished. A day later, the editor of *The Times* wrote: 'We prefer to take our chance of cholera than be bullied into health...There is nothing a man hates so much as being cleaned against his will.'

Assessment of Chadwick's reforms

In the short term, Chadwick failed to bring about widespread improvements. Most town councils chose to ignore the Public Health Act of 1848.

However, health did improve in places like Liverpool and Darlington, where improvements were made to water supplies and sewerage systems. In London, 83 miles of new sewers were built between 1858 and 1875. This was part of a scheme designed by Sir Joseph Bazalgette.

Further reforms

Public pressure for change continued to grow as a result of several influences:

- **Dr John Snow** showed that there was a connection between disease and drinking water. In 1854 there was another cholera epidemic in central London. Snow mapped the areas to see where most cholera victims lived. He found that the worst cases were around the Broad Street water pump. Snow persuaded the authorities to remove the handle of the water pump and, soon after, the outbreak of cholera stopped.
- In 1865–66 more **cholera** outbreaks occurred.
- The **Reform Act** of 1867 gave the vote to working men in towns. This meant that they could now put pressure on politicians to clean up towns.
- By the late 1860s, there was greater understanding of the work of **Louis Pasteur** and more people were aware of the connection between filth and disease.

Public Health Act, 1875

All these things helped lead to the **Public Health Act (1875)**. This made it compulsory for town councils to:

- provide proper systems of water supply, drainage and sewerage for local residents
- appoint a medical officer of health to ensure that this was done

The 1875 act was a turning point in the history of public health in Britain. It led to:

- much cleaner towns and cities
- the end of diseases like cholera and typhoid
- the end of the old policy of laissez faire — from now on, it was widely accepted that governments and councils had to take responsibility for public health

Artisans Dwelling Act, 1875

Further progress was made by the **Artisans Dwellings Act (1875)**, which gave local councils the power to clear slum areas. Someone who had worked hard to create this reform was **Octavia Hill**, a campaigner for better housing for the poor. In the 1860s she had bought up houses, made them clean, and rented them cheaply to poor families.

The situation in 1900

By the end of the nineteenth century:

- The policy of laissez faire had disappeared; governments at both national and local level accepted that they had a responsibility to maintain public health.

- The worst slums had been replaced by better housing, and all towns and cities had proper water supplies and sewerage systems. These developments were greatly aided by advances in **engineering and technology**, such as the introduction of methods of filtering water. Many cities also had public parks and street lighting, and were becoming more pleasant to live in.
- However, although people lived in cleaner environments, hundreds of thousands of them still lived in terrible **poverty**. Lack of money meant that it was impossible for some people to have a healthy diet or afford a decent home. Over the next century, the emphasis shifted towards improving the health of individuals.

In the early 1900s, two factors helped to persuade more people that direct help should be given to poor families:
- **War.** During the Boer War in South Africa (1899–1902) it was found that 40% of those who volunteered for the army were unfit to serve. This seemed to place the security of the whole country at risk. What if there was a major war in Europe?
- **Individuals.** Many wealthy people at the time were against giving direct help to the poor. They believed that the poor should help themselves and be independent; and they believed that the real cause of poverty was laziness. This belief was challenged by two men who studied the causes of poverty in different cities. The research of **Charles Booth** in London and **Seebohm Rowntree** in York showed that the true causes of poverty were things like sickness, long-term unemployment and the death of the main breadwinner. Their work helped change public attitudes and in 1906 a new government was elected which was committed to social reform.

The Liberal governments, 1906–19

Several reforms were passed by the Liberal governments of the early twentieth century:
- 1906: local authorities were allowed to provide **free school meals** for the poorest children
- 1907: **medical inspections** were introduced into schools
- 1908: **old age pensions** were introduced for the over 70s
- 1911: the **National Insurance Act** stated that workers earning less than £160 per year had to make weekly contributions from their pay. In return they received free medical attention when ill, sick pay for up to 26 weeks and unemployment benefit if out of work. The man behind this scheme was the chancellor **David Lloyd George**.
- 1919: the **Housing Act** gave local authorities money to build 'homes fit for heroes' — that is, homes for soldiers returning from the First World War. These were the first council houses and they provided far better-quality housing for families on ordinary incomes.

These reforms undoubtedly brought improvements, but throughout the 1920s and 1930s poverty continued to be a severe problem.
- The **Depression** of the 1930s brought massive unemployment. Some workers received unemployment benefit, but most did not. It was hard to keep a family healthy when there was not enough money to provide a proper diet.
- Lloyd George's Insurance Act did not cover other members of the family, so poorer families often went without proper medical attention because they could not afford doctors' fees. Instead, people relied on 'home remedies' and help from relatives.

- Despite the new council houses, thousands of people still lived in slum housing, where illness and disease continued to be problems.

The National Health Service

Two factors played a key part in setting up the **National Health Service (NHS)**: the Second World War and the work of two key individuals.

The Second World War

During the **Second World War**, air raids killed and injured thousands of people. Medical care had to be provided for all, whether or not people could afford to pay for it. This worked well and the belief grew that a similar system should exist in peacetime.

The condition of city children who were evacuated to country areas was shocking and convinced more people of the need for a better health service.

Key individuals

Two **individuals** were particularly important in setting up the NHS:
- **William Beveridge.** In 1942 the Beveridge Report was published and won a lot of support. Beveridge wanted a **welfare state** in which the government supported people 'from the cradle to the grave'. In his 1942 report he said that everyone should be free from the 'five giants': want, disease, ignorance, squalor and idleness. People should have enough money for a healthy life; there should be a free national health system for all; there

should be free secondary education for all (at the time, most people stayed in one school until the age of 14 and then left); people should have decent houses to live in; and everyone should have a job.
- **Aneurin Bevan.** In July 1945 a Labour government was elected with the aim of creating a national health service. As minister of health, Aneurin Bevan fought hard over the next 3 years to get the NHS set up. He believed that the best medical treatment should be available to rich and poor alike.

Opposition to a national health service

Opposition to the creation of a national health service came from **politicians** who believed that it was taking away people's responsibility for their own lives — that they would lose their self-respect if the state looked after them too much. **Doctors** were also opposed to Bevan's aim. They believed:
- The government would interfere too much in medicine: for example, telling doctors what medicines they should provide for their patients.
- Doctors would lose money if they were not paid directly by their patients.

Bevan overcame this opposition by telling doctors that they could still take private patients as well as receiving a fee from the government for each patient on their 'books'.

The creation of the NHS

In 1948 the National Health Service was created. It offered a huge variety of free services: family doctors, dental treatment, maternity and childcare, health visitors, medicines, blood transfusions, ambulances etc.

The intention was that the NHS would always be free at the point where one of its services was needed. However, within 2 years it was clear that the cost of the service was too great a burden. In 1950 charges had to be introduced for prescriptions, and patients had to make a 50% contribution towards the cost of spectacles and false teeth.

A turning point

Despite this, the NHS still represents a major turning point in the history of public health in Britain.

Before:
- Medical care (doctors, hospital treatment) was not free for everyone.
- Healthcare was based on the National Insurance Act (1911), which covered only some workers and did not extend to include their families.

After:
- Everyone — rich and poor — was guaranteed to have a high standard of medical care.
- The principle that the government was responsible for the health of the public — 'from the cradle to the grave' — was firmly established. This was a huge change from the old ideas of laissez faire and self-help.

The NHS today

Since 1950 costs have continued to rise. **New technology** has enabled advances like organ transplants to develop quickly, and more people are treated with **expensive drugs and equipment**. The cost of **maintaining hospitals** and of **training** (and paying) highly skilled doctors and nurses gets ever higher.

The NHS has become a victim of its own success. As people live longer, the cost of caring for them in the future becomes greater. **Waiting lists** for treatment and **closures of hospital wards** have become hot political issues.

Use the information provided, your class notes and your textbook to answer the following questions.

1 Complete the chart by listing the following events in the correct chronological order:
- Reform Act gave working men in towns the vote
- Boer War in South Africa began
- National Insurance Act gave some workers free medical treatment and sick pay
- First Public Health Act
- National Health Service set up
- First cholera epidemic
- First old age pensions introduced
- Artisans Dwellings Act
- Free school meals for some children introduced
- Beveridge Report published

2 Explain how each of these factors led to poor standards of public health in the early 1800s:
a laissez-faire policies
b the effects of the Industrial Revolution
c ignorance

1 Public health: timeline of events

Date	Event
1833	
1848	
1867	
1875	
1899	
1906	
1908	
1911	
1942	
1948	

2a

b

c

Questions

3 What did Edwin Chadwick believe was needed to improve public health in Britain?

4 When was Chadwick's report published and what was it called?

5 Explain two reasons why some people were opposed to Chadwick's ideas for improvement.

6 Explain why each of the following helped to create pressure for a second public health act:
  a the cholera outbreaks of 1865–66
  b the Reform Act 1867

7 Complete the chart, comparing the effects of the two public health acts of the nineteenth century.

8 In what ways had conditions in towns and cities improved by 1900?

3 _____

4 _____

5 _____

6a _____

b _____

7 Nineteenth-century public health acts

	First Public Health Act	Second Public Health Act
Date		
What did the act do?		
Was it successful or not? Why?		

8 _____

9 Besides acts of Parliament, what other developments after 1875 made these improvements possible?

10 Despite these improvements, what problem still remained?

11 How did the Boer War convince more people that direct help should be given to poor families?

12 Why did some people oppose the idea of helping the poor?

13 Describe briefly four steps taken by the Liberal government between 1906 and 1911 to help poor families.

14 When were the first council houses built and why at that particular time?

15 Why did poverty and ill health continue to be problems in the 1930s?

9

10

11

12

13

14

15

Questions

16 What were the main features of the Beveridge Report of 1942?

16

17 How did the Second World War help to convince people that a national health service was needed?

17

18 Explain why the setting up of the National Health Service was opposed by:
a some politicians
b many doctors

18a

b

19 Why could the creation of the National Health Service in 1948 be called a 'turning point' in the development of public health in Britain?

19

Source A

A COURT FOR KING CHOLERA.

A picture published in 1852, showing living conditions in London

Source questions

20 Does Source A prove that the Public Health Act of 1848 was a complete failure? Use the source and your own knowledge to explain your answer.

20

Questions

21 What can you learn from Source B about healthcare before the National Health Service? Explain your answer using the source.

22 How does Source C help you understand the attitudes held by doctors towards the introduction of the National Health Service in 1948? Explain your answer using the source.

Source C

DOTHEBOYS HALL
"It still tastes awful."

A cartoon from 1948 showing Aneurin Bevan introducing doctors to the NHS

Source B

Headaches — we had vinegar and brown paper; for whooping cough — oil or goose fat rubbed on our chests. For mumps we had stockings around our throats and for measles we had tea stewed in the teapot by the fire — all different kinds of home cures. They thought they were better than going to the doctor. Well, they couldn't afford the doctor because sixpence in those days was like looking at a ten pound note today.

Kathleen Davys describes how poor families coped with ill health in the 1930s, quoted in *Medicine for Edexcel* by I. Dawson and I. Coulson, published in 2001

21 _____

_____

_____

_____

_____

22 _____

_____

_____

_____

_____

_____

_____

_____

23 How far does Source D explain the attitudes of doctors shown in Source C? Explain your answer using Sources C and D and your own knowledge.

> **Source D**
>
> If this bill is passed no patient or doctor will feel safe from interference by some ministerial order or regulation. The Minister's spies will be everywhere.
>
> From the *British Medical Journal* (a publication for doctors), January 1946, quoted in *Medicine through Time* by J. Scott and C. Culpin, published in 1996

23

Questions

Extended writing

On separate paper, write your answers to these two questions.

24 Which contributed more to improvements in public health during the nineteenth century — the work of individuals or the work of governments? Explain your answer fully with examples.

24

Guidelines

A very good answer will:

- Describe the work of two or three individuals who made important contributions to public health.
- Explain, with details, that governments also made important contributions (for example, the Public Health Act of 1875).
- Explain that governments were sometimes pressured into taking action and give examples.
- Come to a clear conclusion and support it with reasons.

25 'The introduction of the National Health Service was widely welcomed in Britain.' How far do Sources B, C and D support this interpretation? Explain your answer using the sources and your own knowledge.

25

Guidelines

A very good answer will include:

- references to Sources B, C and D and additional knowledge not in these sources
- an explanation of why the introduction of the NHS did have widespread public support
- an explanation of why some people opposed the NHS
- a supported conclusion that clearly answers the question set

Ambroise Paré

The French surgeon **Ambroise Paré** (1510–80) was the most famous surgeon of his day and in 1575 published his *Works on Surgery*. He introduced two important changes:

- **Treating gunshot wounds.** Before Paré, the usual method was to pour boiling oil into the wound to 'kill the poison'. Paré learned that it was better to make up an ointment of natural substances (oil of roses, egg yolks and turpentine) and spread it over the wound. This discovery was helped by **war** because if Paré had not been a war surgeon, he might never have come across gunshot wounds, and also by **chance** because he only made up this ointment when he had run out of oil. However, **individual brilliance** also played a major part because Paré was able to improvise (invent something) in a crisis.
- **Stopping bleeding after an amputation.** Before Paré, a hot iron was used to seal the wound. This was called **cautery**. Paré found a less painful way to seal the wound — by tying the veins and arteries with a silk thread.

Other surgeons did not always take up Paré's ideas. This may have been for two reasons:

- **Resistance to change.** Many surgeons preferred to stick to the old methods of cautery because this was what they had been trained to do and it seemed to work. Why change?
- **Knowledge of germs and sterilisation did not exist in Paré's day.** It is possible some surgeons tried tying arteries but found that the wound became infected, so they went back to the old ways.

Paré's work was accepted in the long term, but not in the short term, so his discoveries do not really represent a turning point in the history of surgery.

Surgery in the nineteenth century

At the start of the 1800s and right down to the 1840s, surgeons still had three main problems to deal with:

- **pain** — no effective anaesthetics were known
- **infection** after the operation
- how to replace **blood** lost in an operation

These problems meant that operations were feared. Surgery was only used as a last resort and surgeons did not have high status in medicine. Operations inside the body were extremely risky and rarely attempted. Amputations were more successful, but speed was thought essential to prevent death from shock.

Development of anaesthetics

Attempts to reduce or stop pain in earlier times had involved alcohol and opium, but these were ineffective. The development of effective **anaesthetics** (substances which ensure that patients feel no pain in operations) was as follows:

- 1799: Humphrey Davy noticed that laughing gas (nitrous oxide) dulled pain. A US dentist called Horace Wells tried this with limited success, but no one in surgery ever took it up.

- 1845: William Morton (another US dentist) successfully used ether in dentistry.
- 1846: Dr Warren performed the first operation using ether in the USA.
- 1847: A Scottish doctor, **James Simpson**, began to use chloroform in childbirth, following experiments in which he and two assistants had anaesthetised themselves.

Most surgeons welcomed anaesthetics, as patients would no longer have to be held down during operations, but some did not for the following reasons:
- Ether and chloroform were potentially dangerous; it was difficult to know how much to give patients and some deaths occurred from overdoses.
- A small number of surgeons still insisted that speed was the key to good surgery.
- Some had religious objections, arguing, for instance, that pain in childbirth was the will of God.

Queen Victoria used chloroform in the birth of her eighth child in 1853 and this removed a lot of the opposition to anaesthetics. However, the introduction of anaesthetics led to the '**Black Period**' in surgery, which lasted until about 1865–70. This was caused by the second problem: infection.

Development of antiseptics

Now that surgeons could take more time over operations (thanks to anaesthetics), they could take more risks and attempt exploratory operations within the body. This led to more cases of infection and more deaths after the operation. Standards of hygiene were still low:
- Surgeons wore old coats to protect their clothes and these were rarely washed.
- Surgical instruments were rarely washed properly.

In 1847 a Hungarian doctor, **Ignaz Semmelweiss**, tried to reduce infections passed on to women in childbirth, by insisting that doctors washed their hands between patients. He was seen as a crank and ignored.

In the 1860s, **Joseph Lister** read about Pasteur's work on germs and in 1867 began to use **carbolic acid** to kill germs in the operating area. First he soaked bandages in carbolic. Then after 1870 a spray was used. Many surgeons could see that Lister's methods reduced the death rate and followed his lead, but others opposed or ignored his ideas because:
- The carbolic spray was unpleasant to work with.
- Nurses hated the extra work required by Lister's higher standards of cleanliness.
- Many still did not accept the **germ theory** and so did not see the point of it all.

Despite this opposition, Lister's work was a turning point in the history of surgery. It changed the whole approach to cleanliness in hospitals:
- By the 1880s all operating theatres and hospitals were being rigorously cleaned.
- After 1887 all instruments were steam sterilised.
- In 1889 the US surgeon **William Halstead** first used sterilised rubber gloves.

By 1900 surgery was moving towards **aseptic surgery** — having a completely germ-free environment. The first operation on the heart had been performed. Surgeons had high status and now had teams of assistants. In 1895 **X-rays** had been discovered by a German scientist, **Wilhelm Röntgen**. However, the issue of how to replace the blood lost in operations remained a problem.

Surgery in the twentieth century

Development of blood transfusions

Blood transfusions had been attempted in earlier times, but had usually failed because it was not known that there were different blood groups. **Karl Landsteiner**'s discovery of blood groups in 1901 made safe transfusions possible.

This area of medicine was also improved during the First World War. Soldiers were dying from blood loss because it took so long to get them to a field hospital. A method of storing blood cells in bottles packed in ice was developed. It only needed the addition of a sodium citrate solution to make blood usable for transfusion on the battlefield itself.

Methods of storing blood for longer periods were developed in the Second World War and a **National Blood Transfusion Service** was organised. War also contributed towards the development of plastic surgery. During the war, the surgeon **Archibald McIndoe** developed important new techniques for treating RAF pilots who had suffered terrible burns. These are all examples of how **war** has sometimes helped to speed up medical developments.

Operations

Technology has made increasingly complex operations possible:

- Developments in **aseptic surgery** have made operating theatres totally germ-free.
- **New equipment** has been introduced, such as electrocardiogram (ECG) machines (1903), artificial kidney machines (1943) and heart–lung machines (1953).
- **New techniques** have been developed, such as **'keyhole' surgery** and **microsurgery**. 'Spare part' surgery has made **organ transplants** possible. The first heart transplant was carried out by the South African surgeon **Christiaan Barnard** in 1967.

Surgeons also began to specialise — for example, in heart or brain surgery. Nowadays, they are assisted by teams of skilled nurses and anaesthetists.

Problems remaining

As surgery has progressed, the demand for surgical operations has increased. **Waiting lists** for standard operations can be long and the number of people needing organ transplants at any time exceeds the organs available.

Rising costs in the twenty-first century have led to the closure of some wards and even some hospitals.

Cleanliness in hospitals has become an issue with the spread of the **MRSA 'super bug'**. It has been estimated that as many as 5,000 patients die each year as a result of a variety of infections picked up in hospital.

Use the information provided, your class notes and your textbook to answer the following questions.

1 How were the following surgical problems dealt with before Paré?
a treating gunshot wounds
b stopping bleeding after amputation

2 What better methods did Paré develop for dealing with each of these problems?

3 Explain how each of these factors helped Paré make his discoveries:
a war
b chance

4 Complete the chart by writing the following developments in surgery in the correct space. Add the name linked with each development in the third column.
- Sterilised rubber gloves first used in surgery
- Chloroform first used as an anaesthetic
- First ever heart transplant
- First operation that made use of ether as an anaesthetic
- Existence of different blood groups discovered
- X-rays discovered

1a

b

2

3a

b

4 Developments in surgery: timeline of events

Date	Development in surgery	Individual
1846		
1847		
1889		
1895		
1901		
1967		

5 What three problems still existed for surgeons in the early 1840s?

6 What two chemicals were used by US dentists in the 1840s to stop pain?

7 Why did some people oppose the use of anaesthetics?

8 Why did the introduction of anaesthetics lead to the 'Black Period' in surgery?

9 Why did some people oppose the early use of antiseptics?

10 Explain the difference between antiseptic and aseptic surgery.

11 Which was the more important in surgery in the nineteenth century — the development of anaesthetics or the development of antiseptics? Explain your answer fully.

12 State three developments since 1900 which have made blood transfusions safe and readily available today. In each case, say when these developments occurred.

Questions

13 Explain with at least two examples how new technology helped surgery progress during the twentieth century.

13 _____
_____
_____
_____

14 Complete the chart by inserting the person linked with each development in surgery and the date when it happened.

14 More developments in surgery

Development	Individual	Date
Discovered that nitrous oxide dulled pain		
Used ether as an anaesthetic in dentistry		
Tried to reduce hospital infection by insisting on cleanliness, but was ignored		
Her use of chloroform in childbirth eased opposition to it		
Read about Pasteur's work and began to use carbolic as an antiseptic		
Developed important new techniques in plastic surgery during the Second World War		

15 Explain the following terms connected with surgery:
a cautery
b anaesthetics
c antiseptics
d sterilisation
e aseptic surgery

15a _____
b _____
c _____
d _____
e _____

Source questions

16 How does Source A help you understand why operations were feared in the early nineteenth century? Explain your answer using the source.

Source A

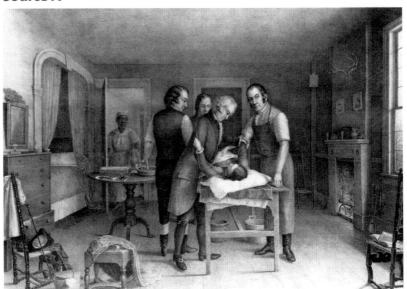

An operation in 1809 to remove ovaries, taking place on a kitchen table

16
_____
_____
_____
_____
_____
_____
_____

Questions

Source B

The effects of chloroform on James Simpson and his assistants

WELLCOME LIBRARY, LONDON

17

17 Study Sources B and C. Source B suggests that Simpson had found an effective means of making patients unconscious during an operation. Source C suggests that this led to further problems in surgery. Does Source C mean that Source B is wrong? Explain your answer using Sources B and C and your own knowledge.

Source C

One would think that the development of anaesthetics would have transformed surgery...There would no longer be the need to complete an operation within a few minutes. Instead of merely amputating limbs, the surgeon could enter the abdominal and chest cavities. But for a time anaesthetics actually created more problems.

From *Medicine and Public Health* by S. Lee, a textbook written for secondary school students published in 2001

18 How does Source D show that operations had changed since 1809 (see Source A)? Explain your answer using Sources A and D and your own knowledge.

Source D

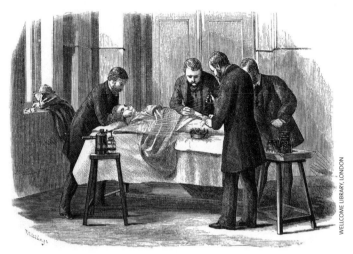

WELLCOME LIBRARY, LONDON

An operation in 1882 using the carbolic spray

18

_____

_____

_____

_____

_____

_____

_____

_____

_____

Questions

Extended writing

On separate paper, write your answers to these two questions.

19 'By the end of the nineteenth century, the problems facing surgeons in the early 1800s had been overcome.' How far would you agree with this interpretation? Explain your answer using Sources A to D and your own knowledge.

20 'The discoveries of brilliant individuals were the main reason for progress in surgery in the period c. 1550–1900.' Do you agree? Explain your answer.

19

Guidelines

A very good answer will include:
- references to at least three sources and additional knowledge not in the sources provided
- explanation of the problems that had largely been overcome (references to Sources A, B and D)
- demonstration that other improvements had been made by 1899 which are not shown in the sources, and that one important problem remained
- a clear conclusion that answers the question set

20 You could include the following in your answer and any information of your own:

- Ambroise Paré found a better way of treating gunshot wounds.
- Joseph Lister began to use a carbolic spray around 1867.
- Robert Koch discovered the germ that caused wounds to become infected in 1878.

Medicine and war

Wars always cause great destruction and terrible loss of life. They can also hinder or damage medical progress. However, in times of pressure and crisis, scientists, doctors and even politicians are often forced to improvise or make inspired decisions that can lead to great medical improvements.

War hindering medical progress

An example of when war has hindered medical progress is the **destruction of the Roman Empire**. During the period AD 400–500, the Roman Empire was attacked and largely destroyed by 'barbarian' tribes from eastern Europe. This damaged medical progress because it led to:

- the gradual breakdown of the Romans' great public health schemes (aqueducts, sewers etc.) — by the year 1000, standards of public health were lower in most towns in Europe
- the destruction of Roman libraries, which led to the loss of many ancient medical texts

War helping medical progress

Here are some examples of when war has helped medical progress:

- In 1536 during the French war with an Italian state, **Ambroise Paré**, the French war surgeon, was treating soldiers' gunshot wounds when he ran out of boiling oil. He was forced to improvise and came up with an ointment made up of egg yolks, oil of roses and turpentine. This proved to be more effective and less painful.

- **Florence Nightingale** and her fellow nurses saved the lives of many soldiers during the **Crimean War** (1854–56). This greatly raised the status of nursing in medicine, and in 1860, with government funds, Nightingale was able to open the first proper training school for nurses.
- In 1870 the **war between France and Prussia** is said to have intensified the rivalry of **Pasteur** and **Koch**, and inspired each man to strive to make new discoveries in their search for greater understanding of **germs and disease**.
- During the **Boer War** (1899–1902) in South Africa, it was found that 40% of the men who volunteered for the British army were unfit to serve. This helped convince more people that reforms were needed to improve **public health** and it was one reason why the Liberal reforms of 1906–11 were introduced.
- During the **First World War** (1914–18) many soldiers were dying on the battlefield from loss of blood. This led to the development of a new method of **storing blood** in a dried form; a sodium citrate (salt) solution was added, which meant that blood transfusions could be given on the battlefield.
- The early years of the **Second World War** (1939–45) brought a huge number of casualties in battle and created an urgent need for a new wonder drug. This led the governments of Britain and the USA to become involved in the development of penicillin. As a result of this involvement, large industrial companies began the **mass production of penicillin**, increasing availability and saving the lives of soldiers in the latter stages of the war, as well as the lives of huge numbers of people in peacetime. During the war, **Archibald McIndoe** learned new techniques for treating the

burns suffered by pilots in battle, and these techniques also became available in peacetime.

Medicine and chance

Sometimes in the history of medicine, things that have affected medical progress have happened by accident, or chance. These chance events have often led to improvements, but on one occasion, in the ancient world, chance greatly hindered progress in one area of medicine.

Chance hindering medical progress

The **Minoan civilisation** flourished in Crete until about 1400 BC when it was destroyed by a volcanic eruption. It was rediscovered in 1900. Excavations showed that the Minoan people had created systems for supplying fresh water and removing sewage over 1,000 years before the Romans began to develop their own systems. However, the destruction of this civilisation meant that, when planning their public health schemes, the Romans had to learn to solve problems that Minoan engineers had already solved. Thus, this natural disaster, a chance event, slowed down medical progress.

Chance helping medical progress

Earlier in this workbook there are some examples of where chance events helped medical progress. Here is a brief reminder of them:
- Paré and a new method of treating gunshot wounds (Topic 7)
- Pasteur and the development of the second ever vaccine — for chicken cholera (Topic 4)
- Fleming and the discovery of penicillin (Topic 4)

However, it would be wrong to think that these discoveries were entirely the result of chance. In each case, other factors played an important part, such as war, individual brilliance, money, new technology and knowledge of previous developments in that area of medicine.

Topic 8   The impact of war and chance on medicine through time

Use the information provided, your class notes and your textbook to answer the following questions.

1 Complete the chart, which summarises the ways in which war has both helped and hindered medical progress.

1 Impact of war on medicine: summary chart

War and dates	Development	Helped or hindered?	How war helped or hindered and names of any key individuals
	Public health	Hindered	
French war with Italian state (1536)	Surgery		Paré discovered a better way of treating gunshot wounds — he used an ointment instead of boiling oil
	Nursing		
Franco–Prussian War (1870)	Germ theory		
	Public health		
	Blood transfusions		
	Penicillin		The urgent need for a new cure led to mass production in the USA. Key individuals — Florey and Chain

Questions

2 Complete the chart to show the part played by chance in medical progress.

Date	Development	Part played by chance	Other factors that helped
	Paré and gunshot wounds		
	Pasteur and the chicken cholera vaccine		
	Fleming and penicillin		

3 Take any **one** of the medical developments in the chart and decide which factor was more important — chance or one of the other factors? Explain your answer fully.

Extended writing

On separate paper, write a short essay in answer to the following question.

4 'A study of the history of medicine shows that wars have done more to help medical progress than to hinder it.' To what extent would you agree with this statement? Explain your answer fully and support it with examples.

Guidelines

A very good answer will include:

- at least one clearly explained example of when war has hindered progress
- at least three fully explained examples of when war has helped progress
- a reasoned conclusion that clearly answers the question set

Before the nineteeth century

From earliest times, women have had at least two important roles in medicine — as **carers of the sick** within the family and as **midwives**. This is an example of continuity through time — that is, of things staying the same. However, there was one short break when, in the eighteenth century, the development of obstetric instruments like forceps led to the replacement of female midwives by male doctors because they, unlike midwives, had been trained in anatomy. Increasingly, women were encouraged to have their babies in hospital rather than at home, but unhygienic conditions there only served to increase what was already a high death rate in childbirth.

Until the eighteenth century, it would have been unusual for women to be treated by a male doctor, primarily because the Church considered it wrong for male doctors to make intimate examinations of women.

In the Middle Ages, poorer women would have relied on the local **wise woman** in the village, who was often skilled in making up herbal treatments. Alternatively, the **lady of the manor** was often expected to treat illnesses and common injuries — in the village as well as among her own family.

In Salerno in Italy, it was possible for a woman to train as a doctor, but this was forbidden in most countries. In Paris in 1322, one woman, **Jacoba Felicie**, was put on trial for treating people without a licence, even though she was successful and well liked

by her patients. She could not obtain a licence to treat people because she was a woman.

The nineteenth century

In the first half of the nineteenth century, the position of women in medicine had hardly changed since the Middle Ages. Women from the poorer classes often went into **nursing**, but nurses had very low status. They received no organised training and had few skills.

It was impossible for women to become **doctors** at this time:
- To be registered as a doctor after 1858 an individual had to pass examinations, but no university in England admitted women, so they were effectively barred from this level of the medical profession.
- A further barrier to women was male prejudice. The prevailing attitudes at this time were that women were psychologically and emotionally incapable of such a complex and demanding occupation and that their place was 'in the home'.

However, progress was achieved in the second half of the century. This was the result of three main factors: outstanding individuals, a shortage of doctors and nurses and improved educational opportunities.

Among the **outstanding individuals** who made significant break-throughs in this male-dominated profession were the following:
- **Florence Nightingale**, who set up the first proper training school for nurses at St Thomas Hospital in London in 1860 with

15 student nurses. By 1901 there were over 3,000 trained nurses working in English hospitals. Nightingale's work in the Crimean War (1854–56) also did a great deal to raise the status of nursing.

- **Mary Seacole**, who was a Jamaican nurse and made an important contribution from 1855 to 1856 to the care of soldiers in the Crimean War, despite a lack of support from the authorities. She even had to pay for her own passage out to the Crimea.
- **Elizabeth Blackwell**, who was born in England but became, in 1849, the first woman to qualify as a doctor in America.
- **Elizabeth Garrett**, who met Elizabeth Blackwell in 1859; she, too, was determined to become a doctor. However, she was refused entry to universities because she was a woman. She had to go to Paris where she qualified as a doctor in 1870. After marriage, she was known as Elizabeth Garrett Anderson.
- **Sophia Jex-Blake**, who studied medicine under Elizabeth Blackwell in New York after 1865. She led five other women in a fight to complete their medical training in Edinburgh. In 1874 she set up the first medical school for women in Britain. Finally, in 1876, a new law was passed by Parliament that made it possible for women to train as doctors in the same way as men.

The second main factor was a **shortage of doctors and nurses**. After 1858 the General Medical Council (GMC) was set up. The GMC laid down much stricter rules about the training of doctors and the examinations they needed to pass to qualify. This meant that the number of qualified doctors went down for a time. Meanwhile, the development of anaesthetics and antiseptic surgery in the 1850s and 1860s created a need not just for more nurses, but for more skilled and better-trained nurses.

The late nineteenth century also saw **improved educational opportunities**. Schooling became compulsory for everyone after 1870 and gradually the universities began to open their doors to women, so more were able to get the qualifications needed for training as doctors.

The twentieth century

Throughout the twentieth century, the number of women in medicine rose steadily. The First World War greatly increased the need for nurses in France and they made a huge contribution to the care of wounded soldiers. Today, nursing is a respected and popular profession, if still relatively poorly paid.

By the 1990s half of all students training to be doctors were women, although senior positions in medicine, such as consultancies, still tended to be dominated by men.

Use the information provided, your class notes and your textbook to answer the following questions.

1 What two roles have women traditionally had in medicine?

2 Why were there fewer females practising midwifery in the eighteenth century?

3 To whom did poorer women turn for medical treatment in the Middle Ages?

4 What were the two main barriers to women becoming doctors in Britain up to the 1860s?

5 Complete the chart by filling in the names of the women responsible for each development and the relevant year.

1 _____

2 _____

3 _____

4 _____

_____

_____

5 Women responsible for medical developments

Development	Individual responsible	Year(s)
First woman to qualify as a doctor in USA		
Outstanding nursing work in Crimean War		
First training school for nurses set up		
Qualified as a woman doctor in Paris		
Set up first school of medicine for women		
Women were allowed to train as doctors		

Source A

Science was now essential for the study of medicine and very few girls learned any science at all. Until the 1850s there were hardly any secondary schools for girls. Even more serious, the world of medical students was an all-male one. They were used to coarse jokes and rowdy behaviour. This was at a time when young ladies of the richer classes were taught to be refined and delicate.

From *Medicine through Time* by J. Scott and C. Culpin, published in 1996

Source B

Elizabeth Garrett (Anderson) passes her doctor's examination in Paris in 1870

MARY EVANS PICTURE LIBRARY

Source questions

6 What can you learn from Source A about the obstacles facing women who wanted to become doctors in the nineteenth century? Explain your answer using the source.

6 _____

_____

_____

_____

7 How far does Source B show that the problems described in Source A had been overcome by 1870? Explain your answer using Sources A and B and your own knowledge.

7 _____

_____

_____

_____

_____

_____

_____

Extended writing

On separate paper, write a short essay in answer to the following question.

8 'The situation of women in medicine had improved by the end of the nineteenth century. This was the result of the work of outstanding individuals.' How far do you agree with this interpretation? Explain your answer using Sources A and B and your own knowledge.

8

Guidelines

A very good answer will include:

- references to the sources and additional knowledge not drawn from the sources
- a description of the work of at least two individuals who overcame problems women faced early in the century
- a description of at least one other factor that helped women make progress
- a summing-up at the end in which you explain briefly to what extent you agree or disagree with the interpretation